Chemtastrophe!

Cleaning Chemistry

Jon Eben Field

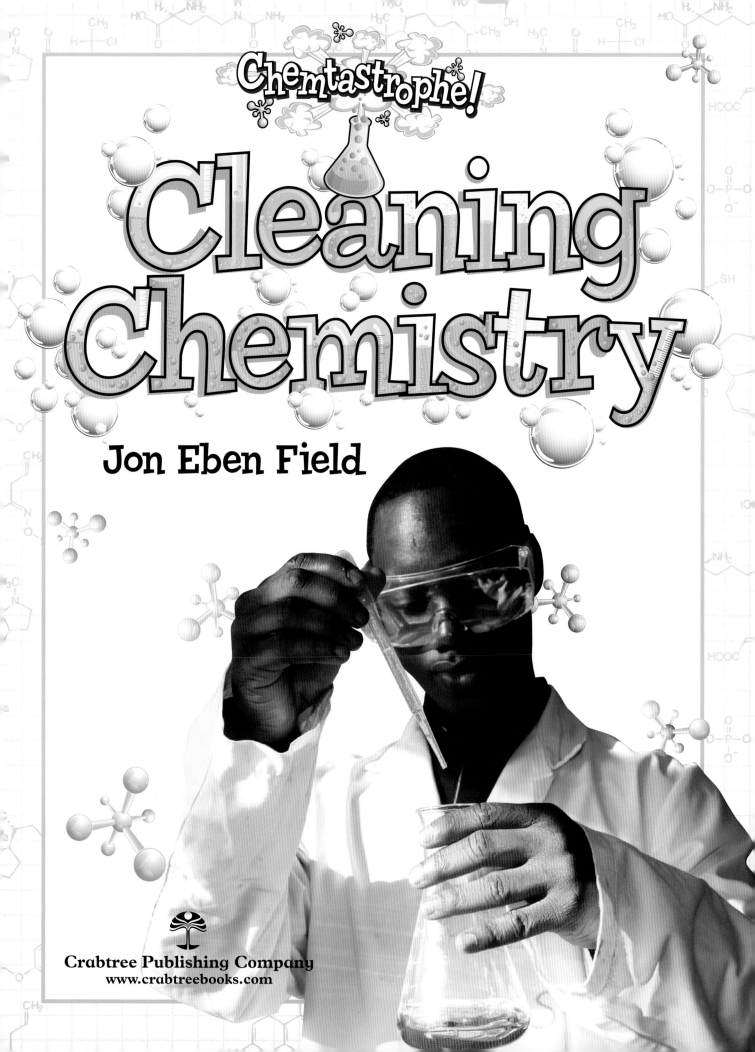

Crabtree Publishing Company
www.crabtreebooks.com

Crabtree Publishing Company
www.crabtreebooks.com

Photographs: Title page: Laurence Gough/Shutterstock Inc.; p.2 : Nobel foundation/Wikimedia Commons; p. 3: Teacept/Shutterstock Inc.; p. 4: Nobel foundation/Wikimedia Commons; p. 5: Jacek Chabraszewski/Shutterstock Inc.; p. 6: Shebeko/Shutterstock Inc.; p. 7: (bottom) Jiri Foltyn/Shutterstock Inc.; (top) Denis and Yulia Pogostins/Shutterstock Inc.; p. 8: Lara Barrett/Shutterstock Inc.; p. 9: Tatjana Melnik/Shutterstock Inc.; p. 10: (top) Georgios Kollidas/Shutterstock Inc.; p. 11: (top) Studio_G/Shutterstock Inc., (bottom) Nobel foundation/Wikimedia Commons; p. 12: (left) Bobbieo/iStockPhoto.com, (middle) Big Pants Production/Shutterstock Inc.; p. 13: (top) Laurie Bar/Shutterstock Inc., (bottom) Granite/Shutterstock Inc.; p. 14: Vlue/Shutterstock Inc.; p. 15: (bottom left) Aquariagirl1970/Shutterstock Inc., (bottom right) Mike Ledray/Shutterstock Inc., (top) Viacheslav A. Zotov/Shutterstock Inc.; p. 16: (bottom left) Roman Sigaev/Shutterstock Inc., (middle) Feng Yu/Shutterstock Inc.; p. 18: (left) Kutlaev Dmitry/Shutterstock Inc., (right) Qju/Shutterstock Inc.; p. 19: Laurence Gough/Shutterstock Inc.; p. 20-23: Jim Chernishenko; p. 24: Slavapolo/Shutterstock Inc.; p. 25: (top) Ashaki/Shutterstock Inc., (bottom) Dominique Capelle/Shutterstock Inc.; p. 26: (middle) Lana Langlois/Shutterstock Inc., (top) Ann Worthy/Shutterstock Inc.; p. 27: (bottom left) Colour/Shutterstock Inc., (middle) Four Oaks/Shutterstock Inc., TFox Foto/Shutterstock Inc.; p. 28: instruct9r/Shutterstock Inc.;p. 29: Chepko Danil Vitalevich/Shutterstock Inc.; p. 30-31: Teacept/Shutterstock Inc.

Publishing plan research and development:

Sean Charlebois, Reagan Miller
Crabtree Publishing Company

Developed and Produced by: Plan B Book Packagers

Editorial director: Ellen Rodger

Art director: Rosie Gowsell-Pattison

Glossary and index: Nina Butz

Project coordinator: Kathy Middleton

Editor: Adrianna Morganelli

Proofreader: Molly Aloian

Prepress technician and production coordinator:

Margaret Amy Salter

Print coordinator: Katherine Berti

Special thanks to experimenter Natasha

"How we know" boxes feature an image of Polish physicist and chemist Marie Curie, renowned for her theory of radioactivity and the discovery of the elements polonium and radium. Despite being denied work in her field because she was a woman, Curie was awarded Nobel Prizes in Physics and in Chemistry in the early twentieth century.

Library and Archives Canada Cataloguing in Publication

Field, Jon Eben, 1975-
    Cleaning chemistry / Jon Eben Field.

(Chemtastrophe!)
Includes index.
Issued also in electronic format.
ISBN 978-0-7787-5284-4 (bound).--ISBN 978-0-7787-5301-8 (pbk.)

    1. Cleaning compounds--Juvenile literature.
2. Chemistry--Experiments--Juvenile literature.
I. Title. II. Series: Chemtastrophe!

TP990.F53 2011   j668'.1   C2010-906580-8

Library of Congress Cataloging-in-Publication Data

Field, Jon Eben.
 Cleaning chemistry / Jon Eben Field.
    p. cm. -- (Chemtastrophe!)
 Includes index.
 ISBN 978-0-7787-5301-8 (pbk. : alk. paper) -- ISBN 978-0-7787-5284-4 (reinforced library binding : alk. paper) -- ISBN 978-1-4271-9609-5 (electronic pdf.)
 1. Cleaning compounds--Juvenile literature. 2. Chemistry--Experiments--Juvenile literature. I. Title. II. Series.

TP990.F54 2011
668'.1--dc22

                              2010042062

Crabtree Publishing Company

www.crabtreebooks.com   1-800-387-7650

Printed in China/012011/GW20101014

Published in Canada
Crabtree Publishing
616 Welland Ave.
St. Catharines, ON
L2M 5V6

Published in the United States
Crabtree Publishing
PMB 59051
350 Fifth Avenue, 59th Floor
New York, New York 10118

Published in the United Kingdom
Crabtree Publishing
Maritime House
Basin Road North, Hove
BN41 1WR

Published in Australia
Crabtree Publishing
386 Mt. Alexander Rd.
Ascot Vale (Melbourne)
VIC 3032

Contents

Science and Serendipity

Do your parents ask you to wash your hands before dinner? You might not like it, but using soap to wash your hands gets rid of dirt and fights—germs. Soap—what it does and how it is made, is an amazing and simple example of the branch of science called chemistry.

Chemistry At Work

Chemistry is a fascinating area of study that plays a role in every aspect of the world around us. Chemistry is all about matter, and matter is anything that occupies space and has **mass**. A bar of soap is matter, but so is an apple, a bottle of soda, or steam rising from a boiling pot. Chemistry is involved in everything we grow, make, and eat. The toothpaste you use in the morning is a product of chemistry. Even the sandwich you ate for lunch was made with bread created through a **chemical** process!

HOW WE KNOW

What is Science?

Science is a method of examining the world around us. We do this by asking and answering questions. Science is based on testing ideas about the world through experiments that are repeatable and produce the same results. Scientists are continually examining things to determine how they work and whether their ideas about them are correct.

Lucky Accidents

Many ideas in science have come about through careful **experimentation**, while others have been "lucky accidents." A lucky accident is sometimes called **serendipity** because of its positive, if unintended, result. Some of the greatest discoveries in science have been through serendipity. It also requires a clever and flexible scientific mind. Scientists have to be able to see the benefits of a lucky accident and understand its possible meanings.

Curious Minds

Scientists ask questions about the world because they are curious. They want to know more about how the world works and why it works the way it does. Training teaches scientists to ask and answer questions in specific ways.

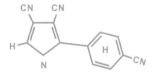

Making food, from bread to sandwich spread, involves chemistry.

Even the toothpaste you use every day is created through a chemical process.

fun fact

Louis Pasteur, the scientist who discovered the rabies vaccine, once said, "In the fields of observation, chance favors only the prepared mind."

Understanding Matter

Matter is in everything around us, from the air you breathe to the food you eat, to the desk you sit at in school.

Mass and Volume

Simply put, matter is anything that has mass and occupies **volume**. Mass is the amount of material in an object. Volume is how much space that object takes up. These are important factors to know and measure when looking at nature and science.

Atoms and Molecules

Matter is made up of **atoms**. Scientists describe atoms as the building blocks of matter. Atoms are tiny structures that are so small they cannot be seen by the naked eye. A molecule is a group of two or more atoms that are stuck together. For example: in the air we breathe, two molecules of oxygen atoms bond together to create O_2. Air is actually a chemical mixture! Molecules can also be made up of different types of atoms.

Periodic Table of Elements

In chemistry, the periodic table is a table of chemical elements, or substances that are the primary parts of matter.

States of Matter

All matter exists in different states. This means matter can be a solid, such as a soccer ball, a liquid, such as water, or a gas, such as vapor or steam. Matter can also move from one state to another. Water is a liquid that becomes a solid when frozen. It can also become a gas when heated. In each of these states, water's molecules change and move differently. As water cools, its molecules slow down and stop moving around. As the water changes into ice, it becomes harder because the molecules hardly move around at all—maintaining shape as a solid. If you heat water in a pot to its boiling point, it will change into a gas. As water is heated, it begins to evaporate. Steam, or water vapor, is water in its gaseous state. As a gas, water molecules move very quickly because of their heat. Water molecules therefore expand as far as they can and fit the space around them.

Water vapor can be seen on a thermal lake and from a boiling kettle.

Scientific Method

The scientific method is a set of rules that guide how scientists observe and test new ideas. Using the scientific method allows people to accurately ask and answer questions about the world around us.

Science as Method

A method is an orderly way of doing things. You probably have a method for storing your clothing where socks go in one drawer and t-shirts in another. When you follow your method, clothing doesn't get jumbled together. In science, method is a process used to investigate, ask questions, and develop possible answers to those questions. Scientific method involves observing things and measuring results, or evidence. Without it, science would be messy and unreliable.

Observing the World

Scientists are always observing the world and asking questions based on their observations. Once a scientist has asked a question, he or she has come up with a hypothesis. A hypothesis is a proposed explanation for how something works. For a scientist, the important thing about a hypothesis is that it is testable. This means that an experiment can be made to determine whether the hypothesis is true or false.

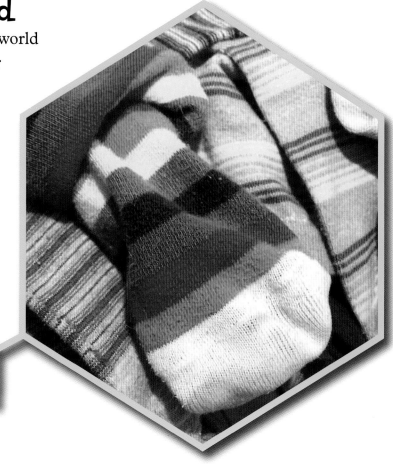

There is a method to the way you store your socks—and to the way scientists investigate things.

Hypothesis to Experiment

In an experiment, the scientist maintains the same environment throughout, but changes one thing called the variable. By changing one thing in the environment, scientists observe and record the results. Being open to observation allows a scientist to see what happens. Sometimes, simply observing with an open mind allows the scientist to capture the magic of a lucky accident. Through **analyzing** the results, a scientist can determine whether the hypothesis was true or false. Sometimes, results are inconclusive, or do not answer the question, and the scientist must go back to the drawing board to refine the experiment.

Method is a way of ordering the world that allows you to see things clearly.

Method Steps

Scientific method involves a simple set of steps to follow:

1. Ask a question.

2. Research to find background information.

3. Construct a hypothesis (a proposed explanation for how things function).

4. Create an experiment to test your hypothesis.

5. Conduct the experiment.

6. Record the results.

7. Determine whether your results indicate the hypothesis is true or false.

8. If necessary, return to a previous step until you arrive at conclusive results.

Theories and Laws

Science also depends on laws and **theories** in order to make observations. Laws are rules for how things work. Although laws rarely change, sometimes new discoveries prove that an old law was wrong.

A theory is an idea about how things work. Theories must be proven by fact. Scientists use theories as a way to see the world around them in a new way. Many accepted scientific laws started out as theories that very few people believed. Through testing and careful experimentation, theories about the world can become laws.

Galileo Galilei was an Italian scientist who used a form of scientific method in his experiments.

fun fact

The ancient Greek doctor Galen encouraged people to use soap for their health over 1,800 years ago. It was not until the beginning of the 1900s that people began bathing with soap once a week.

Method in History

The scientific method started as a series of discoveries in ancient India, Greece, China, and Persia. Pythagoras, an early Greek thinker, used the scientific method to demonstrate that Earth is round. Throughout history, using trial and error and the benefits of lucky accidents, scientists established a set of rules for doing experiments and presenting scientific results.

Pythagoras used science in an attempt to show Earth was round, and not flat as previously thought.

HOW WE KNOW

Ancient Experimenter

A Persian scientist named Ibn al-Haytham or Alhazen is credited with developing the scientific experiment as it is known today. He developed experiments to test how light is seen. By pointing out that light entering a dark room travels in a straight line through dust, he demonstrated that light travels in straight lines.

Everyday Chemistry

Most of the things we do and make in everyday life involve a scientific or chemical process. Normal things like making and eating food, or washing our bodies and clothing involves chemical reactions and interactions, processes where one substance is changed to another.

Changing States

Chemistry is involved in everything we do from the time we get up in the morning until we go to bed at night—and even overnight! Chemistry is at work when you wash your face and hands in the morning. Here is how it works. Have you ever noticed that your hands do not come fully clean if you do not use soap? Well, your hands get dirty because dead skin cells and bits of dirt mix with the natural oils that your skin produces. Oil is insoluble in water which means it cannot be dissolved or disappear. Try rubbing some oil and dirt on your hands. Then wash your hands using only water. The oil does not mix with the water, and the dirt stays on your hand. When you use soap, the dirt and oil are both removed.

Soap removes both dirt and oil.

Lather Up—Soap Works

Soap works because it has two different ends to its long molecules. One end of the soap molecule is hydrophilic, which means "water-loving," while the other end is hydrophobic, which means "water-fearing." The hydrophobic end of soap dislikes water, but is attracted to oil, so when you are washing your hands, this end of the molecule grabs the natural oils that are holding the dirt on your hands and face. The hydrophilic end of a soap molecule loves water, so when you are washing up, this end grabs onto water molecules. This means that when you run water over your soapy hands, the dirt washes down the drain because the hydrophilic end latches onto water molecules, while the dirt is held tightly by the hydrophobic end.

A simple bar of soap is a complex work of chemistry.

Soap History

Soap has a long history, but for most of its **existence** it has been made using the same basic chemical composition. A fat (either animal or vegetable) is mixed with an **alkali** such as lye, which is traditionally gathered from the ashes of a fire. The mixture is then heated.

Traditional methods of making soap took a long time and required a lot of hard work. Today, most soap production takes place in large factories. Some people prefer handmade soaps prepared without harsh chemicals. Most soaps that are produced now are not true soaps, but are **detergents**. One of the problems with true soap is that it reacts with salts or chemicals naturally present in water and leaves a dirty-looking **residue** called a soap film or scum. You may have seen this residue as a brown ring around a bathtub or around the collar of your favorite shirt.

You can't hide from soap scum, but detergents can get rid of it.

fun fact

The first record of soap is a recipe on a tablet from ancient Babylon (now Iraq) almost 2,800 years ago.

Different Cleaners, Different Places

The different kinds of cleaners and detergents we use to clean our homes are all examples of cleaning chemistry. Our kitchens and bathrooms are home to many cleaners, including dish washing detergent, window cleaners, and floor, tub, and toilet bowl cleaners. Even toothpaste is really just a cleaner for your teeth. There are soaps that use powerful chemicals to kill bacteria and soaps made from all-natural ingredients.

Modern household cleaners are chemically designed to do specific tasks, such as clean windows without leaving streaks, or whiten laundry without bleach.

The Science of Clean

When we clean our homes, we use different chemicals based on their properties, or characteristics. Chemists have learned that different molecules, mixtures, and solutions work better at cleaning certain things.

The Emergence of Detergents

The fatty oils used in soaps were in short supply during **World War I**, when world trade and shipping was stopped or redirected. Scientists had to **innovate** and develop new **synthetic** soap-like mixtures. In 1916, the first synthetic detergent was made in Germany. In chemistry, synthesis means creating reactions from two or more materials to make a new product. Chemists mix various compounds, called reactants, and the process creates a new substance. Chemists were looking for a chemical solution that, unlike soap, which cleans best in warmer water, would clean in cold water or even saltwater.

The End of Soap Scum

Synthetic detergents were surface active agents, or surfactants. Surfactants clean by making water "wetter." They lower the surface tension of a water molecule and make the water bind more easily to the oil and dirt trapped in clothing or on skin. The main advantage to detergents is they do not react with minerals in water—eliminating soap scum. In time, chemists began making detergents with specific **properties** that helped soften water, and therefore brighten clothing.

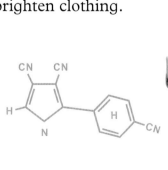

Solvents and Solutions

Many household cleaners are solutions. A solution is something that is **dissolved** in another substance. In a mixture, the substance that is present in the greater amount is called the solvent. For example, when you pour a spoonful of sugar into water, the sugar crystals sit at the bottom of the glass. Give it a stir and you will see that the sugar is the solvent that dissolves into the water, or the solute. The sugary water that results is the solution. When cleaning products are **manufactured**, chemical compounds are dissolved into other substances and liquids in order to achieve the right texture or consistency for cleaning.

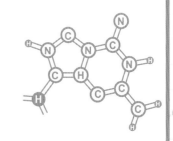

Phosphate detergents clean clothing but they also harm the environment—a chemtastrophe in the making!

Detergent Types

There are two types of detergents: phosphate-detergents and surfactants. Phosphate-based detergents are caustic, which means they burn or destroy things. Phosphate-detergents are particularly harmful to the environment because of how they harm water **ecosystems** by encouraging algae to grow. Bacteria that eat algae then rise in numbers and use up most of the oxygen in the water, making it difficult for fish and other aquatic life to survive. To determine if your dish-or clothes-washing detergent is phosphate-based, check the label.

Let's Test That

An experiment is a set of steps designed to test a theory about how something works. In order to perform an experiment, you must first have a theory.

Testing Theories

A theory is an idea about how something works. For example, your theory might be that dish soap cleans dirty dishes better than laundry detergent. No matter the theory, even if it is simple, it requires testing. An experiment tests a theory by producing results. Results appear when a chemist observes an experiment. When you are performing an experiment, you need to focus on observing because your observations will prove your theory true or false. The results that are produced through observation need to be analyzed. By looking carefully at both your measured results and observations, you can arrive at a conclusion.

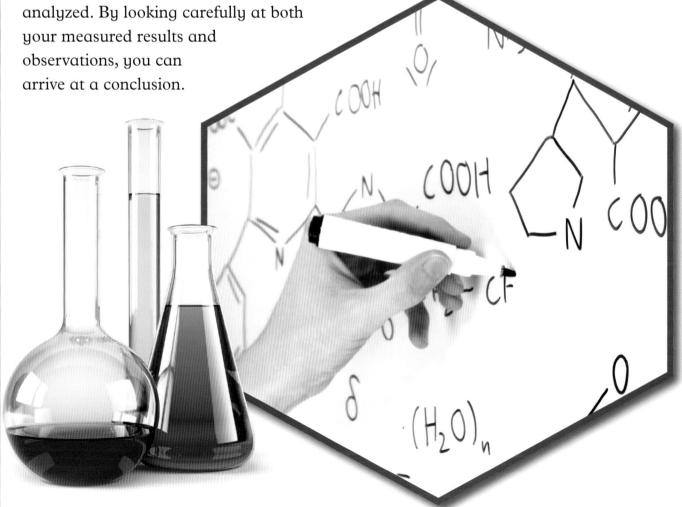

Variables and Measurements

Science experiments are often designed to have variables, or conditions that change the experiment's outcome. There are three kinds of variables: independent, dependent, and controlled. An independent variable is changed by the scientist or experimenter. A dependent variable is altered, or responds, to changes made to the independent variable. A controlled variable is something the experimenter tries to keep constant so that the experiment can be repeated with the same results. Measurement is also key to scientific experiments. Scientists must be able to measure the results of an experiment as well as the variables. Measured results also allow others to read and understand your experiment, hypothesis, and theory.

Making Conclusions

After an experiment, scientists analyze and interpret their results and observations. Scientists want to rule out any other possible explanation for their results. Interpreting results usually involves coming to conclusions, or statements of certainty about the experiment and what was tested.

Chemists are always testing and retesting theories.

You're Soaking In It

Have you ever wondered how dish soap cleans? Dish soap, or dishwashing liquid, is a detergent surfactant mixture that can clean dirty and greasy dishes.

Question: How does dish soap work?

Hypothesis: As a surfactant, dish soap should dissolve oil.

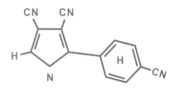

Materials:

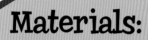

- 4 paper notes
- 4 identical glasses
- 2 teaspoons (10 ml) vegetable oil
- 2 teaspoons (10 ml) dish soap
- water

Method:

1. Write the numbers 1-4 on the paper notes. Stick them to the glasses, or display in front.
2. Fill each glass halfway with tap water.
3. Add one teaspoon of vegetable oil to glasses #2 and #4.
4. Next, add one teaspoon of dish soap to glasses #3 and #4.
5. Using a different spoon for each glass, stir the ingredients for 15 seconds.
6. Make and record your observation of each glass immediately after stirring.
7. Wait 3 minutes and make another observation.
8. Compare your observations.

Ask an adult to help you accurately pour the oil and dish soap onto the spoons.

Stir each mixture carefully.

Record your observations.

Results and Discussion:

Discussion: Explain what you see.

Results: Glass #1 (just water) should stay the same. In glass #2 (oil and water), you should see the oil at the surface of the water, while in glass #3 (water and soap) the soap mixes easily with the water and there may be some bubbles. In glass #4 (water, oil, and soap), the oil should dissolve in the water because the dish soap acts as a surfactant.

Which Washes Better?

If you have ever watched a washing machine in action, you will notice that there is a lot of shaking going on. Washing clothes involves more than just adding a detergent to the wash and letting it soak.

Question: What is the best laundry detergent?

Hypothesis: The best detergents dissolve dirt and oil.

Materials:

4 small numbered papers
4 identical glasses
4 identical spoons
4 small pieces of clean fabric (ask an adult to help)
a small amount of dirt
white vinegar
2 types of laundry detergent
water

Method:

1. Write the numbers 1-4 on folded bits of paper and set in front of glasses.
2. Fill each glass halfway with tap water.
3. Add 2 tablespoons of vinegar to glass #2.
4. Add 2 tablespoons of detergent #1 to glass #3.
5. Add 2 tablespoons of detergent #2 to glass #4.
6. Prepare the pieces of fabric by rubbing a small amount of dirt on each one.
7. Add one piece of dirty fabric to each glass.
8. Stir each glass for 30 seconds.
9. Remove the pieces of fabric and rinse in clean water (remember to keep track of which glass the fabric came from).
10. Observe each piece of fabric and record your observations.

Carefully spoon out the detergent needed and add to glasses of water.

Add the dirty fabric to the glasses then stir the fabric around.

Observe and record your results.

Results and Discussion:

Discussion: Which piece of fabric was the cleanest? Were any of your observations surprising?

Results: Fabric #1 (only water) should still have some dirt on it. Fabric #2 (water and vinegar) will likely be cleaner than #1, but will have a strong vinegar smell. Fabric #3 & 4 should be similar in how clean they are. If either one is far cleaner, tell your parents to buy that detergent!

Eureka! I Found It!

A "eureka moment" is a sudden realization that a solution to a problem has been found or an unexpected discovery has been made. Science is full of eureka moments because scientists are constantly asking questions and searching for answers.

Accidental Discovery

Eureka is a Greek word meaning "I have found it." Ancient Greek scholar Archimedes is believed to have exclaimed this when he noticed that the volume of water in a bath increased when he stepped into it. Archimedes then realized that the volume of water displaced in his bathtub was equal to the volume of his body. This solved the problem of determining the volume of irregular objects—something ancient scientists and scholars did not previously understand. Moments of lucky insight or discovery do not happen that often in science, but when they do it leads to greater understanding of the mysteries of science. Sometimes, scientists set out to discover one thing, but through luck (good or bad), chance, and keen observation, they discover something else.

Ancient Cleaning

The history of cleaning products owes a lot to serendipity. Who knows what drove early humans to mix together animal fats and ashes to create soap? The word soap comes from Latin, the language spoken by ancient Romans. Romans were famous for their cleanliness—both for themselves and their homes. Roman cities had large public baths where people would wash, often with olive oil and strigils, or scrapers, but occasionally with a soap mixture. In Europe, during the Middle Ages, bathing was less common. People feared it because they thought it made you ill. For centuries, bathing with soap was unusual. Now that's a chemtastrophe!

Hygiene to Housecleaning

The **commercial** production of household cleaners began with the same companies that produced soap for bathing. Chemists worked in the laboratories of these companies, creating new formulations for products from toothpaste to floor cleaners. Many household cleaners such as dishwashing liquids and detergents and the plastic bottles they are sold in, are made from petrochemicals. Petrochemicals are chemicals made from oil and natural gas, which chemists synthesize.

Propylene, or propene, is a waste product of oil and gas refining, and a raw material for producing soaps and cleaning products.

Keeping clean involves more than just water.

Chlorine and Bleach

The desire for bright white clothing is thousands of years old. In ancient times, people used the bleaching power of the sun or soda ash, made from burned seaweed, to whiten cloth. In 1774, Swedish chemist and pharmacist Karl Wilhelm Scheele discovered an element called chlorine while experimenting with a mineral ore called pyrolusite and hydrochloric acid. Chlorine is used as a disinfectant and keeps swimming pools clean. Its discovery paved the way for the creation of chlorine bleach, now used to whiten and disinfect things. Scheele's experimental chemistry work led to many discoveries, but also caused his death, likely from mercury and lead poisoning. Like many early chemists, he did not realize many of the compounds and elements he worked with were dangerous.

Chemists must always be aware of how different substances interact. Mixing some substances can create a chemtastrophe!

fun fact

Bleach is used to whiten everything from paper to wood and disinfect things such as toilets and needles. Bleach is a product of chemistry, made industrially by mixing chlorine, caustic soda, and water in a specific way.

Ammonia

Ammonia is an odorless gas and a chemical compound. Among its many uses, it is a building block for making many cleaning products such as window and oven cleaners. Ammonia is found in nature in many forms. The human body even **secretes** ammonia in the kidneys as a natural acid **neutralizer**! Chemists have been synthesizing and producing ammonia since the early 1900s. Today, it is one of the most-produced chemicals, yet it can be deadly if used improperly or mixed with other household cleaners or chemicals. Ammonium nitrate, a form of the chemical compound, is used as a farm fertilizer, and is highly explosive—something some early chemists sadly learned by accident.

Workers wear hazmat suits at an ammonia leak. Dozens of deadly chemtastrophes have happened because ammonium nitrate, used in some fertilizers, caught fire or exploded when improperly stored.

Creative Chemists

Chemists perform many different tasks. Some chemists work in manufacturing, developing new products. Some are researchers in universities, analyzing substances and teaching new scientists. Others work in the mining, biotechnology, **pharmaceutical, or fertilizer industries.** Chemists are at work pretty much everywhere!

What Do Chemists Do Again?

Chemists are able to synthesize, new or useful substances by combining different elements and molecules. Using their knowledge, chemists can make new substances in the same way that you can build a tower out of bricks. They also use their imaginations to create models and theories that explain why chemicals and substances behave the way they do.

Chemists who work in the drug-making business use their knowledge to develop drugs that control pain and fight disease.

In North America, a chemist is a scientist who specializes in the science of chemistry. In some areas of the world, especially Britain, the term chemist refers to a pharmacist, or someone who understands and dispenses medicines.

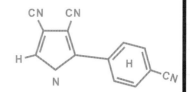

The Future of Cleaning

The chemistry of future cleaning is here, and it is called nanotechnology cleaning. Nanotechnology works with **atomic** and molecular structures that are 100 nanometers or less. One nanometer is one billionth of a meter (3.2 feet). Researchers are now using their knowledge of chemistry to create, for example, a coating that makes toilets and windows self-cleaning.

Chemistry is an ever-expanding field of science.

Want to Learn More?

Chemistry is always going on around you. From photosynthesis in plants to cars burning gasoline in their engines, everything is connected on some level to chemistry. If you want to figure out how things work, understanding chemistry is a great place to start. Here are some resources that will guide you in your exploration.

Chemistry Websites:

Rader's Chem4Kids!
www.chem4kids.com/index.html
A fascinating website that offers an introduction to things like atoms, molecules, reactions, and much more. Games and quizzes are also available on the site.

Strange Matter
www.strangematterexhibit.com/index.html
An exciting and interactive website that looks at chemistry and matter. With both educational videos and fun games, there is something for everyone here.

The Open Door Website: Chemistry
www.saburchill.com/chemistry/visual/PT/001.html
This resource provides an interactive version of the periodic table. By clicking on an element, you can learn a lot about the structure, function, and uses of specific atoms.

Try Science
www.tryscience.org/home.html
Learn trivia, find cool experiments to do at home, and watch live video of scientific projects on this kid-central website.

Chemistry Books:

Why Chemistry Matters series. Crabtree Publishing, 2009. This series uses common examples from everyday life to help explain basic chemistry.

Chemistry by Dr. Anne Newmark: Dorling Kindersley, 2000. This book has ample and varied information on topics in chemistry that are presented both thematically and historically.

Step into Science series. Crabtree Publishing, 2010. Each book in this series explores a step in the scientific method.

Science Fun at Home by Chris Maynard: Dorling Kindersley, 2006. This fun book has more than 100 experiments that you can perform at school or at home.

Cool Chemistry Concoctions: 50 Formulas that Fizz, Foam, Splatter & Ooze by Joe Rhatigan, Veronika Gunter, and Tom La Baff: Larch Books, 2007. Another book of fun household experiments.

Places to Learn More:

Chemical Heritage Foundation
Philadelphia, Pennsylvania
The Chemical Heritage Foundation is an organization devoted to sharing the history of and importance of chemistry through exhibits, events, and education. Check out its website at: www.chemheritage.org

The Museum of Science and Industry
Chicago, Illinois
This museum features a coal mine, a model railroad, a German submarine, as well as a NASA spacecraft used in the Apollo 8 mission.

National Museum of Natural History
Washington, DC
One of the greatest museums in the world, where visitors are free to explore many different exhibits if science, technology, and natural history in the various halls of this large museum complex.

Glossary

alkali A chemical compound that neutralizes acids

analyzing Examining carefully and in detail to identify causes, key factors, or possible results

atomic Relating to atoms

biotechnology The use of living organisms or their products to modify the health or environment of humans

chemical A compound or substance produced by or used in a chemical process

commercial Something made for sale to the public

detergents A water-soluble cleaner

dissolve To incorporate something into another solution or make it disappear

ecosystem A certain area that includes all the living and non-living things

existence The state or fact of existing; being

experimentation The process of testing something to demonstrate a fact

innovate To introduce something new

manufacture The making of goods or wares on a large scale

mass The quantity of matter as determined from its weight, that something contains

neutralizer A solution that is neutral or shows no marked characteristics

properties Essential or distinctive attributes of qualities of a thing

residue Something that remains after a part is removed, disposed of, or used

secretes Discharging or producing a liquid

serendipity A desirable discovery that is happened upon by accident

synthetic Compounds formed through a chemical process made by humans

theories A system of ideas intended to explain something

volume A mass or quantity of something

World War I An armed conflict which took place in Europe from 1914-1918 where Britain, and France and their allies defeated Germany, Austria-Hungary and their allies

Index